Plant Peace Daily

Everyday Outreach for
People Who Care

By Rae Sikora and Jim Corcoran

Plant Peace Daily

Copyright © 2011 by Jim Corcoran and Rae Sikora

Cover photo: Peace Lilies

Proofreader: Lia Rosen

Publisher: Plant Peace Daily

Table of Contents: Page

Introduction   5
Outreach and Activism   6
Inviting Not Fighting   7
The Perfect Venues   8
Communication Tools   11
Outreach on Your Own   21
    Letter Writing   22
    Email Activist Campaigns   30
    Write Articles   32
    Social Networking   33
    Email Signature   34
    Post Comments to Articles   35
    At Work and Leisure   37
    School Activism   38
    Your Car as a Billboard!   39
    Your Body as a Billboard!   42
    Broadcast Veganism   45
    Be a Presenter   46
Outreach on Your Own or
With a Group   51
    Leaflet   52
    Distribute Starter Kits   55
    Create a Local Group   59
    Monthly Film and Discussion   61
    Use Local Public Access TV   62
    Ask-a-Vegan Table   63
    Food Sampling & Literature   64

Natural Food Store Tour 65
Library Displays 66
Host Potlucks 72
Host Speakers 74
Work with Government 75
Educate Clergy 76
Use Local Media 80
Influence Local Businesses 81
Meals for Influential Locals 83
Vegan Meals for Homeless 84
Sticker Around the World 85
At the Beach or Park 86
Stock Veg Starter Kits 87
Quotation Slips 88
Traveling 91
Carry Literature 92
Improve Magazines 93
Deplaning Conversations 95
Influence Restaurants 96
Motels and Hotels 98
Funding Your Outreach 99
Literature and Posters 100
Send Us Your Ideas! 101
Book Testimonials 102
The Authors 104

Introduction

In 2006 we (Jim and Rae) met at a conference and our decades of positive outreach/activism combined and became more than the sum of our parts. Together, our activism spans over 60 years of trial and error. We have learned what about our two very different outreach styles works and doesn't work and why. We have been so pleased with the success of our combined efforts that we started offering a workshop to share our ideas with others wanting to do positive outreach in their communities. The workshops and handouts were so wildly popular that we knew it was time to put those ideas together in an easy to use book that people could refer to whenever they were ready to be an active, positive, educating force in the world. Most of the outreach we have been doing has been focused on vegan, animal, health, human rights, environmental and consumerism issues. We hope that this book will help you take that extra step in helping those without a voice. Your activism and outreach will be part of co-creating a more compassionate world. Thank you to everyone who supported and inspired us on our individual and joint paths.

www.PlantPeaceDaily.org

Outreach and Activism

If you ask most people to describe an activist they will describe someone protesting angrily on the street. We cannot count the number of times we have heard someone say *"I want to be an activist, but I hate protesting."* Protesting is one of thousands of ways to educate and bring attention to an important issue. While we recognize that protesting can often be an effective tool for raising awareness, we do not include it in this book. What we do include is lots of inviting "vegucation" (vegan education) outreach tools.

Inviting Not Fighting

Each of the ideas in this book is a variation on inviting those around you to the possibility of co-creating a world with less suffering and violence and more caring and compassion.

Whether you are an introvert or an extrovert, you will find the perfect fit for your own positive outreach here on these pages. Some of the ideas, like leafleting, require approaching people. Other ideas, like tabling, require being present and letting interested people approach you. Some of the ideas require good listening and other people skills. Other ideas done via the internet or post do not require people contact. Consider your personality and comfort level with each of these to determine which outreach avenues work best for you.

Most of the outreach activities require no specialized skills or big bucks. For those that do require some funding, we have included sources for potential funding.

The Perfect Venues

Finding the perfect locations and events for your outreach will become easier with time. Here are some guidelines:

Find the places where people congregate. Ideally you want the general public and not those already familiar with your ideas. Preaching to the choir is not only a waste of time and resources, but will leave you feeling less effective in your outreach goals.

LOOK FOR PLACES WHERE LARGE NUMBERS OF PEOPLE ARE:

...BORED - This includes anyplace where people are waiting in line, or waiting long hours for various forms of transportation, entertainment or appointments.

...GATHERED WHO CONSIDER THEMSELVES EDUCATED OR PROGRESSIVE - This includes people who are part of the peace and environmental movements. The umbrella of peace is growing and is starting to include all cultures, species etc.   Be part of this growth by doing outreach to this group.

...ARRIVING AT OR LEAVING A LARGE EXHIBIT, CONCERT, LECTURE OR MOVIE.

Wouldn't they love to read something?

Communication
Tools

A few tips for creating a positive experience for you, your group and all who hear your message.

When you are doing outreach, you are really saying, *"Want to be part of my community?"*
Who wants to be part of a community that makes them feel like they are a bad person?
Who wants to be part of a community of unhappy, tired people?
Who wants to be part of a community that isn't fun?

Answer: NO ONE!

Be a bright, healthy, positive example in all your outreach. Get plenty of sleep, eat healthy foods, meditate, do yoga, go swimming, go hiking…..do whatever it takes for you to feel balanced, joyful, alive and vibrant. Then go do your out-reach.

Learning about environmental devasta-tion, violent treatment of other species and health issues inherent in animal ag-riculture affects each person differently. People's reactions range from despair and sadness, to anger and rage. When dealing with despair, it is important to, whenever possible, surround yourself with other caring people who know the issues and understand what you are feeling.

In addition to looking at how far we have to go, it is helpful to look back at how far we have come. We are at the forefront of a social change movement. It is not that long ago that slavery, child labor and women not being part of government were the norm in the USA. In hindsight, everyone would want to be able to claim that they were on the "right side" of those changes. The reality is that the vast majority of people were apathetic or against those positive changes. A dedicated vocal minority tipped the scales.

It is also important to celebrate the victories. There was a time when the word, "vegetarian", and the concept of it, were quite foreign to most people. Now it is known by pretty much all people. The word "vegan" is showing up on packaging and restaurant menus, worldwide. We have a hard time keeping up with all the vegan blogs, publications, celebrities, storefronts, online business, restaurants and organizations. This is good news for us, two people who used to think they knew every vegan in North America!

For many people the social isolation of making a choice that is different than the choices made by friends and family is devastating. We may learn what is happening and want to shout it from rooftops. It is hard to understand why everyone isn't on board with us when they learn the realities, too.

Remember that for most of us there was a time when these ideas were completely foreign and new. If it took you 30 years of your own experiences to get to where you are now, do not expect the people you are connecting with to "get it" in five minutes. Also, remember there are ways that you are still evolving and learning about ideas that you have yet to be exposed to. These ideas are still "around the corner" for you. Be patient with yourself and others. Everyone around us is both our teacher and our student.

Strive to understand rather than trying to be understood. You can do this by asking others questions about their choices. This will not only help you understand them better, but give them an opportunity to examine their own choices in a supportive environment.

COMMUNICATION EXAMPLES:

Someone tells you that they are a vege-tarian who eats fish. (It happens a lot). Rather than telling them that fish is not a vegetable or all the reasons you don't eat fish, find out how they came to that choice. You can ask them:

"How did you come to the conclusion that you would include fish in your diet but not other animals?"

"It can be confusing for people to hear that you call yourself a vegetarian when you eat fish. What makes you want to describe yourself as a vegetarian?"

~

Someone comes up to your table and says, *"I just eat chicken because they are so stupid. But, I don't eat other meat."* Rather than having to go into every study on chicken intelligence or discuss the fact that intelligence is not a measure of worth, you can say something like: *"I have a very different experience of chickens. Tell me about your experience with chickens."* The chances are very slim that they have any direct experience of a live chicken.

~

Someone asks you if it is ok if they eat meat once in a while. The easiest way to answer this is to simply ask them:
"Is it ok with you? This is something you need to come to terms with on your own. If it doesn't fit your values of compassion/non-violence it is probably not the best choice for you."

~

Keep in mind that you are there to invite, not fight. When someone approaches you and wants to argue about the issues, remember that you do not need to engage in negative exchanges. You can simply say: *"I would love to discuss these important issues with you, but only if it will be a calm discussion where we can both be heard."* If the person does not want to calmly discuss the issues, you can walk away after making it clear that you are not interested in arguing.

Sometimes the same question said in two different ways can have two different meanings. For example, if someone says, *"Why don't you eat eggs?"* They may genuinely want to know, or they may be saying, *"It is ridiculous that you do not eat eggs."* The simplest way to discern their motives is to say: *"Would you really like to know? If you would really like to know, I would love to share my decision-making process with you."*

~

Recently, Rae got an email announcing that a radio host was going to be interviewing Sally Fallon on her show. Rather than writing to the host and chastising her for even considering interviewing someone who promotes dairy products, Rae chose another option. She wrote the following to the radio host:

Dear _____
I know that many people follow Sally Fallon's teachings and diet recommendations. What I would like you to be sure to ask her about is the "animal compassion" element. No matter how "humane", "raw" or "organic" a dairy labels itself, the milk is being stolen from the calf it is intended for. I have seen the dairy cows bellowing for their male calves being taken to slaughter (males are a "byproduct" of the dairy industry). I have seen these same mothers pressed against the barbed wire until they bleed as they try to get to their babies. I have watched the same with goats. Please try to get Ms. Fallon to address the necessary theft of babies and milk, the premature slaughter of the mother cows and the killing of the young males in all dairy operations. Thank you so much.

The radio host wrote a wonderful email back and said that she agreed with all that Rae wrote and would definitely ask the guest to address these issues.

She was able to keep the doors of communication open by expressing an invitation to a possibility, rather than making the host feel wrong for having this guest. It made all the difference.

~

It is very common for carnists to say "Sorry I am eating meat in front of you" when a vegan shows up. Many vegans respond to this by saying, "Don't be sorry to me, be sorry to the cow (or pig, sheep, goat, chicken)," While this sounds like a reasonable response, it often comes across as very sharp toned and the doors of communication are closed. It is much more effective to simply ask "Why?" or "Why are you sorry?" This gives this person an opportunity to examine their own motivation and they will possibly come to the most compassionate conclusion on their own.

Outreach On Your Own

IDEA: Letter Writing (even if you can't :)

Writing letters to newspapers, businesses, and legislators is powerful outreach. (If writing letters is challenging for you or you don't have time to compose one, go to the end of this article for a quick and easy way to participate).

When you write letters to the editors of local newspapers you reach thousands of people! Also, most government officials assume that one letter represents hundreds of constituents who have the same views but have not written.

Some tips for letter writing:

*Read local papers and magazines for fuel for letters. Watch for articles, ads, or letters that mention animals, health, and the environment. Some examples: ads for rodeos, circuses, and fur stores, articles about medical experiments, cancer/heart disease/obesity, features about local humane groups or companion animal care.

*Letters don't have to be rebuttals. Circus in town? Noticing a lot of strays? Write a letter. Or use the calendar for inspiration: At Easter, tell readers why they shouldn't buy bunnies or baby chicks. On Mother's Day, remind your community of the animals whose babies are taken from them for the dairy industry, animal experiments, zoos and aquariums.

*Write about good news, as well as bad. Thank the paper for providing vegan recipes, or its coverage of a protest or an educational event, or for running profiles of animals available for adoption at shelters.

*Be brief! Sometimes one short, well-written paragraph is enough. Try to stay well under 300 words (about one typed page). Editors are less likely to print long letters.

*Type, if possible. Otherwise, print legibly. Be sure to use correct grammar and spelling, and remember to have it proofread. You can often type and email your letter rather than sending a hard copy.

*Make sure you include your name, address, telephone number and email address with your letter. Some newspapers verify authorship before printing letters.

*Look for opportunities to write op-ed pieces for local papers. These are longer articles of about 500 - 800 words that summarize an issue, develop an argument, and propose a solution. Send the article to the Editorial Page editor.

*You can also write (or call) television and radio stations to politely complain about their slant in coverage of non-human animal awareness or to compliment them on a program well done.

SOME TIPS ON STYLE

*Increase your credibility by mentioning anything that makes you especially qualified to write on a topic: For instance; *"As a registered dietician, I have seen effects of …,"* or, *"as a mother,"* or, *"as a former fur-wearer,"* or, *"as a cancer survivor,"* etc.

*Try to tell readers something they're not likely to know. Give them a peek behind closed doors/gates with your writing and encourage them to take action in their personal lives.

*Whenever appropriate, include something for readers to do beyond their personal choices.

*Keep grudges and name-calling out of letters; they'll hurt your credibility.

*Whenever possible use affirming, positive, inviting language. Educate about the possibilities and empower people to be part of that co-creation.

*Don't assume your audience knows the issues.

*Inclusive language helps your audience identify with you.

*Use positive suggestions rather than negative commands.

*Personalize your writing with anecdotes and visual images.

Avoid speciesist language. Instead of referring to an animal with an inanimate pronoun ("it"* or *"which"*), use *"she"* or *"he."*

Avoid euphemisms ("negative reinforcement," "culling the herd"*); say what you really mean (*"painful electric shocks," "slaughtering deer"*).

*Criticize the cruelty, not the newspaper.

SOME EXAMPLES OF WORDING THAT MAY IMPROVE THE EFFECT OF YOUR LETTER:

EXAMPLE: *"How could people be so uncaring and thoughtless? Only violent, backward people would support something like this."*
BETTER: *"Most caring people would stop eating meat if they saw the conditions in which the animals are raised, trucked and slaughtered. Most people are unaware of the process that brings their food to the grocery."*

EXAMPLE: *"Don't support the cruel veal industry."*
BETTER: *"Calves factory-farmed for veal are first taken from their mothers (dairy cows) at only a day or two old and then tethered in small stalls, kept in complete darkness and fed a low-iron diet. Many people do not realize the connection between the dairy and veal industries."*

EXAMPLE: *"Eating meat is bad for your health."*
BETTER: *"Once people learn about the many negative health effects of eating*

meat, the next step is to act on what we know. We can support each other in making healthy, compassionate choices."

EXAMPLE: *"Don't go to the circus."*
BETTER: *"As people learn the truth about animal circuses (including violent training and suffering in transport), many are choosing to support more compassionate, human powered circuses, such as Cirque du Soleil."*

EXAMPLE: *"Leghold traps can trap an animal by the face, leg, or stomach."*
BETTER: *"Have you ever seen a yearling fox with her face caught in a leghold trap? I have, which is how I know traps tear into an animal's face, leg, or stomach."*

EXAMPLE: *"There is no excuse for your article promoting the circus."*
BETTER: *"There is no excuse for the abuse that goes on in the circus."*

(Some of the information included here is from:

http://www.peta.org/actioncenter/letter
-writing-guide.asp)

**** Another useful tool is to subscribe to the online version of your local newspaper. Articles come up regularly that you can comment on. Comments are usually submitted at the end of the story. Post links to other articles that support your assertions. Educate the people in your area!

Note: Jim composed a letter and made sure that it was concise, timely, empowering and met all the criteria for publication (especially length). He then submitted it online to the target newspaper and to newspapers in other cities of the region. His letter to the editor went into six different newspapers with total readerships in excess of one and one half million. The op-ed page of the newspaper is the second most read section, after the front page. If, conservatively, ten percent of the readers read the op-ed page, that would be 150,000 people that read his letter! He hasn't talked to 150,000 people total, in all of the presentations he has done over the past ten years. Yet, with one well written letter, he was able to reach many more mainstream people with only a little effort and help influence public opinion. At the very least, you will educate the editor of your local paper and he/she will likely be more open to your point of view for future articles. "Letters to the Editor" are well worth the effort! P.S. Save your letters and submit them to other publications, or, months later, to the same one, if not published before. Minimize work and maximize effect!

Note: For those of you who would like a quick and effective way to participate go to: http://www.farmusa.org/letters.htm and sign up to submit letters someone else has written. If you can't write one yourself, use this powerful shortcut!

IDEA: Email Activist Campaigns

Many organizations offer prepared emails to government officials, CEOs and others needing guidance around animal and vegan issues. None of these groups send a consistent vegan message, but many of their pre-formed emails, will help tip the scales (culturally and financially) toward a society that is more inclusive, healthy and compassionate.

Membership is not required to participate in their email campaigns and you can pick and choose which emails to send.

Try it and decide if it is the right method for you. You can opt out at any time. Here are some groups and links you may want to consider:

-The Center for Biological Diversity
http://www.biologicaldiversity.org/actio
n/activist/index.html
-Humane Society International

http://www.hsi.org/action/
-The Humane Society of the United States
http://www.humanesociety.org/action/
-People for the Ethical Treatment of Animals
http://www.peta.org/action/action-team /default.aspx
-Organic Consumers Association
http://salsa.democracyinaction.org/o/64 2/t/6488/signUp.jsp

Note: Links change frequently!

IDEA: Write Articles

Do you love to write? Find publications that are always looking for articles. You do not have to be a published author to submit articles.

EXAMPLE:
Newsletters are often searching for contributors. Check out the local food co-op, religious groups, student groups, health clubs, neighborhood associations, etc. If they have a newsletter, offer to write articles for them.

ANOTHER EXAMPLE:
Research submission guidelines for various magazines. Once you have read the actual magazine and feel that your article is appropriate for their audience, submit your piece using their guidelines. It is always a good idea to have at least one other person read your article before submitting. You would be amazed how input from a different perspective will improve the effectiveness of your article.

IDEA: Post on Social Networks

Use on-line social networks such as Twitter, Facebook, Linkedin, etc. to get your message out to others.

Once you get used to being part of these networks, you can learn to use them efficiently to reach thousands of people. You can share articles, links, on-line videos and photos, book and movie reviews, etc.

EXAMPLE:
When there is a showing of an important film or any other event that you want to help promote, you can share it in one click on Facebook. The link will be incorporated into the info that you share and the reader can just click once to get more information.

IDEA: Email Signature

Use your email signature to get information out to the world.

EXAMPLE:
Set up an automatic signature for the bottom of every email that you send out. It can include quotes, links to videos, organizations, blogs and articles... or anything you want to promote. Most people will be curious enough to check it out and if they like it, they will pass it on to others. If you include a link to graphic footage, many people will not open your links again. So, it is better to have positive, empowering messages about what one person can do. One of our favorite messages is:
Check out this uplifting and inspiring video on why people choose vegan: http://veganvideo.org

You can also add or use a message from a group, like Peaceful Prairie at this link: http://www.peacefulprairie.org/signatures.html

IDEA: Post Comments to Articles

Post comments at the bottom of on-line newspaper and magazine articles, blogs, etc.

Many people spend hours each day reading the feedback comments after articles. Use the same style tips listed above for letter writing.

Note: Don't get caught up in the heated exchanges of some online posters. They aren't likely to change and replying to them is a waste of time and energy.

EXAMPLE:
An article in an internet version of a Florida paper dedicated 7 pages to Earth Day, but not one mention was made about animal agriculture. Jim wrote a comment after the article and generated a lot of discussion of the issues.

Yahoo and Google offer a service to search for the words like health, envi-ronment, vegan, vegetarian or animal rights online and they deliver them to your email inbox every day. Go to the links and post your brief comment. At the very least, the author will learn something!

Again, try a simple message like this: *Check out this uplifting and inspiring video on why people choose vegan: http://veganvideo.org/*

Note: Educating writers, bloggers and their readers by this means is very effective. It's quick and simple and goes a long way to making lasting change.

IDEA: At Work and Leisure

Get a reputation as the one who brings delicious healthy treats to your workplace, book group, hiking group, writing group, or the gym. Even if you don't like preparing food, you can get already prepared foods and share those along with literature.

EXAMPLES:
Rae hosted a weekly writing group at her home and served homemade vegan cookies and tea at each gathering. A few of the group members joined the local veg group.

Adena is one of our favorite vegan activists and she has vegucated countless people (including co-workers who went vegan) with her delicious baked goods. She brought treats to her staff weekly and left literature in the office for anyone to read.

IDEA: School Activism

See your classes as an opportunity to educate other students or your instructors. An educational institution is a place where everyone is both teacher and student. Speeches, written essays, and other projects can often have compassionate living incorporated into their themes. Include simple vegan samplings of non-dairy milks and cookies with your projects, when possible.

For those wanting to visit schools as a presenter, you can get humane education training through various groups including:

www.humanesociety.org
www.humaneeducation.org
www.nahee.org
www.teachhumane.org

You can also find humane education ideas in the Sowing Seeds Workbook (get a free download at www.teachkind.org).

IDEA: Your Car as a Billboard!

Bumper stickers are great...

This one and others stickers can be found at PlantPeaceDaily.Org

...but even better is a magnetic sign or a design screened right on your car. If you think you are going to want to sell your car at some point, stick with the magnetic sign idea.

EXAMPLES: While we are on the road full time, we are a slow moving billboard on the highway.

The back of the travel trailer we tow has this on the back:

The side of our truck has this sign:

Our friend and fellow vegucator, Susan Hargreaves, has screened images and messages on two cars:

For inexpensive, high quality custom magnetic signs (like the one on our truck) you can go to a local sign maker in your area or order on line through a number of easy to use, on-line printers such as: http://www.vistaprint.com

IDEA: Your Body as a Billboard!

Rae used to fight this idea. She just wanted to wear clothes that didn't say anything on them and cruise anonymously through airports and other crowded places. But Jim insists she wear the black vegan shirt sold at www.veganshirt.com. It is a bit of a text heavy message for people to read, but once they start, they usually manage to read the whole thing. Even if no one approaches you or talks to you when you are wearing the shirt, it educates people about the existence of a compassionate living movement. It is also important that if you are wearing a vegucation tee that you look healthy and have a positive attitude.

EXAMPLE: While going through the security line at the Atlanta airport, someone yelled to Rae: *"Hey Vegan! Hey Vegan!"* She looked all around through the hundreds of people in the lines and found the happy shouting person who had his two thumbs up in the air and a huge smile. When she saw him he yelled, *"Me TOO!"* Everyone around Rae stared at the shirt and read the whole thing. She then put her daypack and shoes on the moving belt and went to the other side. As she was flipping her pack over her shoulder, someone gently slid it off her shoulder. She turned around to see a bright-faced twenty something security worker who was now holding her bag and said, *"I want to finish reading. Can you step over here so people can get through?"* He read the whole shirt and, with such sincerity, said to Rae, *"I am vegetarian. Is this the next step for me?"* She asked him why he was vegetarian. He said it was for compassion and non-violence. Rae told him that this was the inevitable next step for him. *"Thank-you"*, he beamed at her.

At another airport, an employee ran out of a retail store and asked Rae if she had the time to come in for a few minutes. When she and Rae got in the doorway of the store, the woman asked, *"Are you really vegan or just wearing the shirt?"* *"I am really vegan"*, Rae answered. The young woman then said, *"I am vegetarian. I would like to be vegan. I just don't know what to eat."* What followed was an hour long conversation on how this woman could easily make the leap from vegetarian to vegan. Curious co-workers and customers were all involved in the conversation.

Human billboard!

IDEA: Broadcast Veganism

Almost everyone has a Wi-Fi router at home and can make better use of it. Rename your Wi-Fi to VeganVideo.Org and everyone in your neighborhood, condominium complex or apartment complex will see your link. If you have a local veg group you can promote them or any link you want. Dozens of people (or more!) will see it as one their internet options and many will be curious enough to check it out the website.

IDEA: Be a Presenter

There are many groups that are hungry for people to do presentations. Community service clubs, adult education, after-school programs, schools, religious groups, TOPS (Take Off Pounds Sensibly), Elderhostel and many more are looking for people to present programs that encourage critical thinking around current issues.

Are you someone who gets nervous speaking in front of people but you would like to get over your fear? Try joining a group like Toastmasters. You will not only get lots of practice and great feedback, but you will have a regular audience for topics that you care about.

Many people think that they have to be an expert in some area to do a presentation. A presentation can be as simple or detailed as you want it to be. You ARE an expert when it comes to sharing your own experiences. Often, a simple program of sharing some part of your life experience is the most powerful. If you want to present on any issue that you feel passionate about, you can do research and in the process learn more about it for your own education as well.

EXAMPLE: Rae and Jim are often asked to share the path that led them to living a life that is focused on compassionate choices. A simple program that Rae often leads for schools and churches is simply called "I Love Animals". It is a presentation filled with questions for the audience. They are asked *"How many of you LOVE animals?"* Most hands go up. She then asks them to share who is included in this caring. *"Which species?"* When they only share a few companion animals and some wildlife, she asks them to explain why others are not included. It turns into a lively thought provoking discussion.

Rae also does programs related to ethical consumerism and peace. Programs in these categories appeal to a broader range of hosting groups and include compassionate vegan choices.

Jim does a program on phytonutrients because most people do not know about these plant-based food powerhouses. Even people who are not that interested in health issues love learning about something that is basic to our everyday lives and that we know little or nothing about. Jim also does a program called "Caring for Home" teaching people about the connection between their dietary choices and environmental degradation.

You can learn to love doing presentations!

Outreach On Your Own or With a Group

IDEA: Leaflet – pass out literature at colleges or large public events.

There are so many wonderful veguca-tion publications that are available free or for very little cost. See the resources section at the back of the book for a list of publications/organizations and ideas for covering the cost of the literature.

Although we have included this in the On Your Own or With a Group section, it is much more effective with at least one other person. As a friend of ours in Michigan put it, *"One person handing out literature on a street corner looks like a crazy person, two or more people look like an organized movement."*

EXAMPLE:
Vegan Outreach is one of the best groups to contact for literature and ide-as. They have a peaceful army of peo-ple leafleting all over the map. They target universities because this demo-graphic is the most open to new ideas

and are formulating how their values and their lifestyle will fit together.

Passing out literature is probably not the most glamorous or the most appealing work someone could do for a cause. However, if taken seriously, and done on a college campus, it is an extremely effect means of outreach for the time, money and energy expended.

It doesn't require you to know all the issues or to devote a lot of time. It is simple and once you have done it for about a half hour, you become an expert. No more fear of rejection or confrontation. Most students simply take the booklet and leave.

Now, if you distribute say 500 booklets over the course of 2 hours and if only 2-3% of the students actually are moved by the literature and make a change, then you will have helped transform 10-15 students! If every activist did that once a week, we would create a more compassionate world in no time.

This is also a great way to get the word out about your own local organization by stamping/stickering your groups contact info on the back of the material you are distributing.

ANOTHER EXAMPLE:
We took *A Life Connected* booklets to Atlanta for a free talk by the Dalai Lama. 10,000 people attended in a large park. When the talk ended we handed out many hundreds of the booklets. We simply stood at the exits and offered them while saying *"Free nonviolence philosophy booklet?"* How could they resist? And we just know the Dalai Lama would have had no issue with the caring message in each one since it fit his talk perfectly!

Leafletting = big rewards!

IDEA: Distribute Starter Kits

EXAMPLE: Gather old issues of veg magazines, DVD's, cd's of podcasts, brochures and/or recipes and assemble in large envelopes. Create an on-line listing on Craigslist.org (in the Free section) and Freecycle.com. Write a brief ad: Free Vegetarian Starter Packets! You can also list them in your local food co-op newsletter classifieds and the bulletin board in your local natural food store.

We have gotten emails from folks expressing their gratitude for the kits.
Here are a three of those emails:

"It was actually pretty serendipitous that you offered those packets on Freecycle. I had been thinking about it for a long time and just in the week previous to your email it had been particularly on my mind. I had been behind a truck with the bumper sticker, 'Peace Begins in the Kitchen,' for quite some time one day that week and, though a bit cheesy, it really struck a

chord with me that day (it was Rae and Jim's vehicle she saw the bumper sticker on!) *Anyway, we have been meat-free a week now and have switched to soymilk. I feel lighter and peaceful. Hopefully we will be moving more towards vegan in the next several months as I figure out what works and what doesn't in so far as cooking meals for my daughter and me... Any tips on what products are good and tasty would be great, esp. egg, butter, and cheese substitutes, and other dairy products that we use often?"*

"A very sincere thank you for your activism and for giving us the final push. It hasn't been long, but at this point I can't see myself going back... :) Tanya"

Note: Tanya became vegan and went on to take over editing the local coop newsletter and is now writing a column in it titled "VeganMomIcon!"

~

"It has been a few months since my husband Mark picked up one of the free

vegetarian starter magazines from you, but I wanted to give you an update! I read the magazine and started gearing myself up to go veg. I did a lot of research and in continuing on my ever expanding quest to care for animals, our planet, and my own body as well, I made the switch to vegetarian! Jackie"

~

"I just wanted to let you know that you helped me to build the 'know-how' to go vegetarian with confidence and to say thanks so much for handing these out to those who want them! I actually have been thinking about finding out if I can get a stack of them to give out to other people, too (not on freecycle, but friends and interested customers and folks who ask about how I'm doing veggie). I would like to have them available at my store to give away when it feels like a customer is interested (not ever pushy)!

I have been having so much fun with my vegetarian cooking and I not only feel great about my body and health, but my heart and spirit feel at peace with not hurting my animal friends.

Again, I just wanted to say hello and give you thanks and an update. I happened to see your post on Freecycle today for a veggie thing again and it reminded me that I could let you know how you helped create a positive change for me! :) Love, Jennifer"

We have received many more email thank you letters…. but you get the picture.

IDEA: Create a Local Group

No community is too small for a local group. You will be pleasantly surprised at the number of people who show up and join your events, if the group and events are inviting and positive. You can form a local group around any special interest (veg families, veg singles, vegan athletes, etc)

EXAMPLE: Start a Meet-Up.com, Facebook.com, Yahoo.com or any of the other online groups. These online community networking tools are often the place people go when they first get to a community or when they have a specific interest and want to find others who share that interest. You can cover the initial set up cost and then ask for donations from members at various events (this will easily cover the initial set-up cost).

Some Veg Meet-Up groups are called Vegetarian and still ask that members please only bring vegan items to potlucks, so that everyone can enjoy everything. Successful Veg Meet-Up groups have had dine-outs at restaurants, potlucks, cooking demos, hikes, DVD discussion nights at someone's home, movie nights at theatres, etc.

💡 IDEA: Monthly Film and Discussion

These can be done at local community centers or community rooms at natural food stores, churches, schools, etc. They often have a projector. Watch garage sales for portable movie screens or borrow one each month for venues that do not have one.

EXAMPLE: When Rae moved she noticed that, in the middle of town, there was a large community center with a brand new LCD projector hanging from the ceiling. When she inquired, she found out it was available for no charge. She showed environmental and vegucation films each month. The community center would be standing room only because there was really not much else to do in the evenings in her little community. Each film was followed by lively discussions.

Note: Funding for a different type of Video Outreach may be obtained from VegFund.org.

IDEA: Use Local Public Access TV

Many local public access channels allow residents to show educational films. Take your favorite DVDs (Eating, The Cove, Sharkwater, The Witness, Peaceable Kingdom, etc.) to their offices and request that they be scheduled into the programming (It's likely that you will not get a great time slot, but any is better than none).

You may also be able to produce your own local access TV show. It requires some training, but you and/or your group could have some great fun vegucating your community. You could invite national vegan celebrities who are visiting your community to be guests, have cooking demonstrations, etc.

IDEA: Ask-A-Vegan Table

This was Jim's idea and it has been a huge success at stores across the USA.

EXAMPLE: Make an appointment with the manager of your local natural food store. Offer to set up a table at the store with samples of vegan foods that they sell (most will provide the samples free of charge). Make a nice big sign that says *"Ask a Vegan"*. Display literature and answer questions that people have about vegan choices. The first store Jim did this for loved it so much that he was able to do it four times each year with all the samples provided by the store. He used simple foods that could be replenished on the spot. Some perfect choices are: pre-baked flavored tofu cut into cubes, chocolate soy and almond milk, organic baby carrots and hummus for dipping them in. If your store is not open to providing the samples for free, you may be able to get funding for the food and literature from Vegfund.org.

IDEA: Vegan Food Sampling with Literature

EXAMPLE: Contact the organizer of any event going on in your region to see if they would be interested in free vegan food being served. The event can be anything from an environmental event to a sports event to a shelter adopt-athon to an art opening to a church event. Any place where a large number of the general public are gathered is good. See Vegfund.org for lots of ideas and an application for funds. Vegfund pays for the food, table/booth fee and serving supplies for qualifying individuals/groups and events.

IDEA: Natural Food Store Tour

Anyone new to eating healthy veg food can feel overwhelmed with this new way of shopping and eating. A store tour with a seasoned vegan will dispel myths and make their transition smoother.

You can offer this service through your local veg Meetup group or through your natural food store or grocery. If you lead the tour in a conventional grocery, it will encourage the owners to carry more veg options.

EXAMPLE: Rae and Jim led their first store tour in a large natural food store in Georgia. Individuals paid $10 in advance and were met at the entrance to the store at a specific time. This was a big store and took two hours to go through. Keep this timing in mind as you schedule your own tour. You need this time to be thorough and answer their many questions. You will find that people do not want to leave even after two hours! This is a very fun event.

IDEA: Library Displays

Almost all libraries and colleges have display cases in busy corridors and rooms. They often make these available free to the public and are grateful for anyone who will put the effort into creating an educational and creative display. This is an opportunity to display your veg books, magazines, photos and other materials as well as promoting any veg friendly books the library stocks. If you include items that are attractive to children, they will bring their parents over to the case.

Display cases reach the many people who would never consider approaching a table or a person.

EXAMPLE: Jim filled in excess of 75 cases over eight years in the Detroit metro area and rescheduled them quite often. Every day, hour after hour, the exhibits were doing outreach work. Here is how it plays out: Say a library is open 12 hours a day for 5 days a week for 4 weeks. That would be 12x5x4= 240 hours. So for 2 hours work, your reap 240 hours of outreach in your own town. You can't beat knowing that the display is hard at work while you may be goofing off!

HOW IT'S DONE:
If the community you live in is large enough, there may be several libraries (or branches) and a college or two within a short commute for you. Check your phonebook and start calling. Find out who is in charge of scheduling the display case. Allow at least 2 or 3 months to schedule a case because demands may be high. However, we have often called and gotten in immediately. Usually you get the case for an entire month starting on the first and ending on the last day of the month. Incidentally, don't bother scheduling a case for the months of November and December. These holiday months are typically very slow for libraries.

Be prompt and friendly. Bring some cruelty-free cleaning products to prepare/clean the case for your display.

Always leave the case better than you found it. Bring tape, a stapler and tacks.

Each case is quite different, from size to style. You can make it very elaborate or as simple as displaying a few of your favorite vegetarian books (the library may even let you use copies of their books). If you're looking for things to display contact vegan/vegetarian and animal rights groups for ideas. They can be very helpful. Don't use anything that could be objectionable or offensive. Remember your goal is to invite people to a positive possibility rather than make them feel so bad for what they are currently doing that they won't even look at the display case.

Some Library Display Resources:

DISPLAY POSTERS
11" x 17" display posters (set of 3) No S&H! $1
http://www.veganoutreach.org/advocacy/resources.html#displayposters

DISPLAY PHOTOS
8.5" x 11" prints 10 enlargements with captions for display $20
http://www.veganoutreach.org/advocacy/resources.html#displayphotos

Choose Health
http://pcrm.org/shop/pcrm/index.html

Note: These links change frequently, so be prepared to look around and do other searches. There are lots of materials out there to use for little expense.

Here are some letters of appreciation Jim has gotten from librarians:

~

"We'd like to thank you for doing a vegetarian display during May at our library. I saw many of our visitors stop and look at the case with interest. Both the circulation staff and the information desk staff mentioned that residents asked for more information. Thank you again for being willing to share your

'passion'." Sincerely, Library Programs Specialist

~

"Thank you so very much for filling our showcase with fascinating materials about vegetarianism. The display is of great interest to our library patrons. Thank you for sharing it with us." Sincerely, Library Director

~

"Just a little note to let you know how many patrons in our library stopped by to see your display on vegetarianism. It really sparked an interest in our community. I personally benefited from the material having a daughter who declared herself a vegetarian at age 4, saying 'I can't eat anything with a face!!' Thanks again." Sincerely, Adult Services Librarian

Note: Jim has had many librarians consult him as to what vegan books to order for the library. An educated librarian helps educate the public!

Note 2: An easy way to promote your local group or to offer free literature is to cut the top off of a favorite soymilk or almond milk carton, wash and dry it, fill it with free literature and then attach it to the glass of the display case with a suction cup or two. It works great and having some takeaway is vitally important for patrons to follow-up on when they leave the library newly inspired.

One of many styles of cases.

IDEA: Host a potluck, picnic or meal at a restaurant

Make this a fun event by creating a colorful flier and making it inviting for everyone (children, carnists, vegetarians, vegans, seniors).

EXAMPLE: Are you discouraged by holidays that feature a carcass in the middle of the table? Time to create your own holiday traditions! If you do it as a potluck, no one has to be overwhelmed with making all the food and everyone who is new to compassionate eating learns something from creating a plant-based dish. One thing that they may learn is that they already eat plenty of vegan dishes. Include your contact info for anyone who has questions. If they can't figure out what to bring, ask them about their five favorite dishes to create. Inevitably one of those is vegan. It may just require a small change like substituting a non-dairy spread like Earth Balance for the butter. If the caller is someone who uses the internet, you can tell them to Google the name of their dish but add "vegan" to the search. They will most likely get thousands of recipes to choose from! The first large community Thanksgiving that Rae created in a tiny rural village attracted 60 veg and non-veg people of all ages. It was called a Living Thanksgiving. She had a corner of the hall set up for kids to make art projects and there was music and dancing after the meal. The event started with a large circle of everyone holding hands and saying one thing they were grateful for. A man in the circle said, *"I am grateful that no living beings were needlessly slaughtered for this meal."* Everyone brought their recipe written out and set it next to their dish.

The possibilities are endless for creating compassionate potlucks and holiday celebrations.

IDEA: Host Speakers

Any community or group that you are part of would benefit from a local or national vegucation speaker doing a presentation for them. Neighborhood associations, religious and spiritual groups in many communities are looking for speakers on a regular basis. Some well-known national speakers charge little or nothing to come to your region and do presentations. While they are in your area you can set up interviews with the local media and find other local group venues like Rotary, Lions, TOPS (Take Off Pounds Sensibly), libraries, universities etc. Most speakers are willing to stay in your home.

Tip: When hosting a speaker in your home, make sure you remember to give them plenty of quiet re-charge time, healthy food and lots of water.

IDEA: Work With Local Government

EXAMPLE: Ask your city mayor or town supervisor to sign a World Vegetarian Day proclamation. For more information: http://www.worldvegetarianday.org/youcando

Another possibility would be to ask your local government to ban animal circuses or carnivals using animals. This action can pre-empt traveling "slave" shows before some unthinking group invites them in. Here's a how to link: http://www.circuses.com/ADBform.asp

IDEA: Educate Local Clergy

Of all the people with influence in your community, you would think that a compassionate lifestyle would be a given for clergy. Unfortunately, in most cases, they are unaware of the violent nature of animal agriculture. So take the time to educate them!

EXAMPLE: Jim has done this outreach two different ways. You can either sit down at your computer and get the names and addresses of all the local places of worship and mail them each a "Would Jesus Eat Meat Today?" booklet (and/or the DVD "A Sacred Duty") or you can ride around (preferably by bike) and drop one or both of them off at the door or mailbox. Whatever way you choose, just be sure to do it. It's time to stir the conscience of these community leaders! Here's a link to get the booklets:http://www.allcreatures.org/cva/books.htm and to get DVDs ("A Sacred Duty" is great for a Christian audience too), send an email to president@JewishVeg.com and explain your plan and request a specific number.

ANOTHER EXAMPLE: A great form of outreach is to print up copies of "Peace on Earth" and mail them to local churches after Thanksgiving (and well before Christmas). On the envelope to the church, add at the bottom, "Sermon Idea!" to catch the attention of the clergyperson.

Here is the text for "Peace on Earth". A colorful PDF version is available at: http://plantpeacedaily.org/files/Peace_on_Earth.pdf

~

The following is a revised version of a poem by author C. David Coates. Please view this as an invitation to look at everyday inconsistencies from a fresh perspective.

"Humans.....

They kill wildlife - birds, deer, all kinds of cats, coyotes, beavers, groundhogs, mice and foxes by the million in order to protect their domestic animals and their feed.

Then they kill domestic animals by the billions and eat them. This in turn kills people by the millions, because eating all those animals leads to degenerative - and fatal - health conditions like heart disease, stroke, kidney disease, and cancer.

Then humans spend billions of dollars torturing and killing millions more animals to look for cures for these diseases.

Elsewhere, millions of other human beings are being killed by hunger and malnutrition because food they could eat is being used to fatten domestic animals.

Meanwhile, few people realize the inconsistencies - we kill so easily and violently, and then plead for 'Peace on Earth.'"

The good news is that each of us has the power to choose compassion. We can make choices that fit with our most life affirming values. These choices care for other humans, our own health, as well as the health of the planet and all species. Please visit these websites to help align your core values with your actions: http://veganvideo.org & http://tryveg.com

~

Note: Don't forget to make extra copies to post to community bulletin boards. You may also want to send it to editors, family and friends by email or snail mail. Posting to online peace and religious forums is a good use of your time, too. Be creative, even use it year round.

IDEA: Use Local Media

EXAMPLE: Placing ads in local newspapers or other publications can help you reach thousands of people. The ad can be for an event, cause or idea.

Potential advertisement

💡 IDEA: Influence Local Businesses

EXAMPLES: Solicit bookstores to set up a display of vegetarian cookbooks and to offer special discounts throughout the month. If they are open to having food served, you can set up a promotional table with vegan food samples during a busy time in the store. (Remember: Vegfund.org may help you fund this).

-Request vegan products at your local grocery store or a grocery chain. When Rae requested that the local market in her community in Sweden carry the Swedish brand of oatmilk and oat ice cream, the store owner was worried it wouldn't sell. She offered to buy any that did not sell. As it turned out, the community bought up the vegan oat products as fast as the store manager could order them. You might be surprised how many vegans or open-minded eaters live in your community.

-Ask local restaurants to offer vegan options and support them when they do.

When restaurants and grocery stores carry vegan products, those who are not yet vegan will also buy them and inadvertently support compassion.

-Request vegucation books at your local and chain bookstores when you see that they are not carrying some of the better ones. When visiting the store, you can also do a little "public service" display work by rearranging the books in certain sections. For example: If there are cookbooks promoting beef, chicken or fish, you can rearrange things so that the vegan cookbooks are highlighted with the cover showing and the others are back on the regular display shelf. Your display will very likely remain there for a very long time, unless the vegan books sell out!

-Wherever you find comment cards, such as natural food stores and restaurants, take a few and fill them out and submit them for more vegan options. Get friends to do the same!

IDEA: Deliver a Vegan Lunch to Local Officials (with media coverage, if possible) or to Local Radio Talk Show Hosts

EXAMPLE: Visit the local community radio station or public radio affiliate during their show that focuses on environmental issues and bring vegan samples or meal for the whole staff. Once again, you may want to check out Vegfund.org for potential funding.

Note: This one is so easy and the DJs can't help but rave about the food they are eating over the radio. Team it up with an event your group is having and you have a simple inexpensive way to promote the event and educate listeners.

IDEA: Serve Vegan Meals at Area Homeless Shelters

EXAMPLE: Many communities have a chapter of Food Not Bombs and most are vegan. Getting involved with these groups or your local homeless shelters and soup kitchens is a great way to vegucate the staff and those who come for a meal. Be sure to have literature on hand.

Note: It never hurts our cause to clue the media in on your plans. A little good press for veganism is priceless!

IDEA: Sticker Around the World

Bus stop shelters, newspaper boxes, street crossing poles, backs of low signs community recycling bins and public bathroom stalls are all prime locations for vegucation stickers. We prefer the more realistic and less cartoony ones. But any stickers will introduce people to the concepts and raise consciousness.

EXAMPLE: Some countries still have lots of phone booths. You not only reach the person using the booth, but they usually share what they are reading on the sticker with the person they are talking with. When traveling in Spanish speaking countries, take stickers in Spanish and post on poles, signs and public phones.

IDEA: At the Beach or Park

EXAMPLE: If you like to be outdoors and you are healthy, strong, and comfortable in a swimsuit, sundress, or other beachwear, this is for you.   Hit the beach with literature, a wheeled cooler with dry ice and vegan ice cream treats on a hot day. Create a beautiful sign for the side of the cooler and carry literature that you hand out with each free treat.   You can also do this on nice weather days at any park or other crowded outdoor public place. Vegfund.org can also help fund this type of outreach.

Nicecream anyone?

IDEA: Stock Veg Starter Kit Dispensers

EXAMPLE: Get an outdoor newspaper/brochure holder (some groups may be willing to supply the holder). Keep it stocked with veg starter kits from one of the groups in our resources section. These can be placed inside or outside groceries, on busy street corners or other prime locations once you get permission from the manager or local officials. Be sure you keep it full!

Free veg kits

IDEA: Quotation Slips

So many opportunities arise to educate when we are the least prepared. One of the most common is when you go out to eat at a restaurant. We have learned to keep little printed quotation slips with us. They easily fit in a wallet. We have done the layout for you at http://www.plantpeacedaily.org/resourc es.html. You can modify the .doc to include your own favorite quotes or include a website for a local group. If you want to print it up as we have written it (with links to an inspiring video and a free vegetarian starter kit), you will find a PDF on our website. One 8-1/2" x 11" sheet of paper will create 12 slips (front and back)! Take it to a copy shop and print them there. They are better quality (ink won't run) and you can use their paper cutter to make your slips. Below are the two quotes and links we use.

"Nothing will benefit human health and increase chances for survival of life on Earth as much as the evolution to a vegetarian diet."
Albert Einstein   www.veganvideo.org

"The animals of the world exist for their own reasons. They were not made for humans any more than black people were made for white, or women created for men."
Alice Walker, Author Activist   www.tryveg.com

EXAMPLE: A great place to put these little slips is in the sugar tray on restaurant tables. Fold it up and tuck it in front of the sugar packets. After you leave, other diners will surely find it. You will start a table conversation without even being there! These powerful quotes will undoubtedly have those diners thinking about something they never intended when they arrived. And, don't forget to stick one in with the check payment (along with a generous tip) to the wait staff.

Leave these on public bulletin boards, counters, in waiting room magazines, in library books and anywhere you think they would vegucate people! With this form of activism you can afford to leave plenty of them around every single day!

Traveling

IDEA: Carry Literature

Always carry lots of vegucational book-lets/brochures with you (See recommendations in the resources pages of this book). These can be left in the seat pockets (put in the airline magazine, airport chapel (most large airports have them) and even slid into the new magazines in the bookstore as a bonus for buyers! For the chapels, carry "Would Jesus Eat Meat Today?" booklet and/or the DVD, A Sacred Duty.

EXAMPLE: Set the booklets on the seats in the waiting areas of airports, train stations, etc. The seats are rarely cleared off and you will get to watch lots of folks reading them.

IDEA: Improve In-flight Magazines

Use a pen to write inviting vegucational commentary in the on-flight magazine. Find any ads for dairy, meat, pharmaceuticals; etc and let readers know a bit more about the realities. Include websites for information related to health, animals and the environment. It is almost like being instantly published.

EXAMPLE: Rae was on a flight to Ithaca during February (Valentines Day) and had lots of time to write in the magazine. There was an article titled "Romantic Dinners" with meat recipes throughout. On the big white space above the photo of juicy prime rib, Rae wrote: *"There is nothing romantic about a food that causes erectile dysfunction and heart disease. For a truly romantic dinner (and for your health, the animals and the earth), create a healthy plant-based feast. More info at*: (here she included a number of website addresses)." Once she had finished writing on all the ads in her own magazine she traded it out for the magazines of her fellow passengers.

Another great airplane idea: Write with a thin permanent marker on the shiny menu that is in the seat pocket. Write a sentence about the positive reasons to choose plant-based menu items. Then, make a key that lets folks know that vegan items are marked with a V. Go through and mark all the snacks and beverages that are vegan with a V. Again, include websites for more information.

A pocket of potential

IDEA: Engage People in Conversation as you Deplane

EXAMPLE: If there is a delay in getting off the plane and people are getting antsy, you can say something like: *"I used to get so impatient being trapped in here waiting for people to get off the plane. Then I realized that I am here by choice and it is very temporary... unlike the animals who are stuck in cages for their entire lives in puppy mills or laboratories or factory farms. When I think about them having no freedom, this little bit of waiting in here doesn't bother me anymore"* to another waiting passenger. Every time Rae has done this, it has started a very positive conversation. People start talking about their own experience/awareness of animal suffering, etc. You are surrounded by caring people who love to speak up when this topic is brought up. And other people are listening closely. They are a captive audience.

IDEA: Influence Restaurants

Even if you are not hungry and you have plenty of time before or between flights, always go sit down in a restaurant that you know does not have vegan options and ask the wait staff if they have vegan entrées. You can do the same in all transportation centers and as you are walking down the street in town. If you ARE hungry, order the vegan food and request more options for the future. This educates the staff about the concept of veganism when they ask what vegan is. It also lets the manager know that there is a demand for vegan choices.

EXAMPLE: A group of us were walking down the street in a university town. We were on our way to the local veggie café. We were passing an Italian restaurant that has no vegan options and decided to go in and ask if we could see the menu. We asked the host at the door if they had any vegan entrées. He told us they didn't and he and the owner had to watch 8 people walk out the door without ordering. This accomplishes two things: The manager or owner will know that they lost a bunch of potential customers because of the lack of vegan food and the word/choice of veganism is now part of their awareness when it may not have been before.

IDEA: Motels and Hotels

EXAMPLES:

If there is a menu in the room for area restaurants or room service, you can write on them directly and suggest area vegetarian restaurants or suggest the vegan items on the room service menu. Explain why and provide websites for more information. Also, call room service to inquire if they have any vegan options. Even if they don't, they have learned that there is a demand out there. We have gotten several hotel/motels to stock soymilk for their free continental breakfasts, just by asking.

-Leave vegucation brochures tucked into the phone book.

-Slip a piece of paper into the room's Gideon bible or write on the paper edge: Gen. 1:29 - Says GO VEGAN!

Funding Your Outreach
(Funding resources and ideas on getting donated food or literature)

Vegfund.org
Visit this website for food outreach ideas and potential funding. There is an on-line application and the process is fairly simple.

Company/organization donations:

Many food companies are anxious to have people sample their products and will provide either the food samples or coupons. Contact a variety of companies with your well organized outreach plan (including projected number of attendees for the event) clearly expressed and you will most likely get plenty of support.

Many non-profits will provide literature free or low-cost for distributing in your outreach efforts.

Some Organizations Providing Literature and Posters:

http://www.pcrm.org/health/veginfo/vsk/
http://www.veganoutreach.org/advocacy/resources.html
http://friendsofanimals.org/
http://nonviolenceunited.org/alifeconnected.htm
http://www.humanemyth.org/downloads/HumaneMythHandbill.pdf
http://www.peacefulprairie.org/prairiePress.html
http://www.cok.net/market/#pro-veg_literature
http://www.all-creatures.org/cva/books.htm
https://secure2.vegsource.com/farmsanc/item.cgi?rm=edit_item&item_id=864
https://secure2.vegsource.com/farmsanc/item.cgi?rm=edit_item&item_id=614
http://www.veganoutreach.org/advocacy/resources.html#displayphotos
http://pcrm.org/shop/pcrm/index.html
http://www.pcrm.org/shop/cancerproject/rainbow.html

Note: Links change frequently!

Send Us <u>YOUR</u> Ideas!

*If you have proven ideas that should be included in this book, send them to us for consideration for the next edition of **"Plant Peace Daily: Everyday Outreach for People Who Care."***

Contact us through our website www.plantpeacedaily.org or send us an email at book@plantpeacedaily.org

Thank you for all you do to co-create a more compassion planet for all life!

Book Testimonials

"I carry your book with me everywhere I go. I can't wait to get started! I just love your approach, I feel like I finally found the way I want to bring Animal Rights and veganism to light." ~ Mia W.

"... I always thought that I would get into vegan activism after I retired, but now I am realizing that I could start today... Great ideas!" ~ Bonnie Y.

"This is such a great book! It's a gem full of ideas. I bought one at the Animal Rights Conference in July and now I need another because I just gave away the original! Thanks for all you do."
~ Marsha H.

"My husband brought home your book from the NAVS Vegetarian Summerfest. The very first library I called was very receptive to the idea. I'm looking forward to it. Thanks!" ~ June S.

The Authors

Photo by Yvonne Smith

Jim (JC) Corcoran is co-founder of VegFund, Plant Peace Daily and VegMichigan. He is a retired fire captain/paramedic/training officer with a BS in Emergency Medicine and is certified in the Living Foods Lifestyle. Jim is also a certified fitness instructor and a former softball champion/all-star. Jim leads life-altering programs on activism, health and the environment. His talks empower people to make informed and lasting changes in their lives.

Rae Sikora is co-founder of VegFund, Plant Peace Daily and The Institute for Humane Education. Her innovative critical thinking programs have redefined personal power and the ability of one person to make a difference in the world. She has been leading programs internationally for 30 years on compassionate living and all forms of non-violence, including: ethical consumerism, advertising / media influences, communication, conflict resolution, animal rights / awareness, and environmental awareness / responsibility.

Made in the USA
Charleston, SC
08 March 2012